Walking Together As One Flesh

A Marriage Resource For Daily Living

By
Jimmy Mitchell

Copyright © 2016 by Jimmy Mitchell

Walking Together As One Flesh
A Marriage Resource For Daily Living
by Jimmy Mitchell

Printed in the United States of America.

ISBN 9781498494267

All rights reserved solely by the author. The author guarantees all contents are original and do not infringe upon the legal rights of any other person or work. No part of this book may be reproduced in any form without the permission of the author. The views expressed in this book are not necessarily those of the publisher.

Scripture quotations taken from the King James Version (KJV) – *public domain*

Scripture quotations taken from the New International Version (NIV). Copyright © 1973, 1978, 1984, 2011 by Biblica, Inc.™. Used by permission. All rights reserved.

Scripture quotations taken from the New Living Translation (NLT). Copyright © 1996, 2004, 2007 by Tyndale House Foundation. Used by permission. All rights reserved.

www.xulonpress.com

Foreword

---❉---

This book is a must-read to the people of Jehovah God who desire a kingdom of God marriage. Today in the church world, many have gotten a great injustice when it came to marriage counseling of godly couples.

This book will help you establish the marriage God intended in the Garden of Eden if you put to practice what is written.

The Word of God says to "meditate in my Word day and night, then your way will be made prosperous and you'll have great success."

This book, written by my friend and brother in Christ, is filled with God's Word, instruction, and promises.

And I know the Father, by his Spirit, has anointed Pastor Jimmy Mitchell to write this book. Not only has this man of God written this book, but is walking and bearing fruit in his own marriage. Because of countless hours Pastor Mitchell and I have spent on the fishing bank discussing marriage, my marriage has taken a 180-degree turn for the glory of God. I've learned marriage is both people giving our Lord Jesus 100% of ourselves and in return Holy Spirit causes us to give 100% of ourselves to each other in Holy Matrimony.

Thank you Pastor Mitchell for putting 100% of the Father God Jehovah's heart into this book. May He transform every marriage and marriages-to-be into kingdom of God marriages.

Evangelist Michael Peters
Founder: Victorious Way, Truth, and Life Ministries, Inc.
Tucson, AZ

Introduction

———— ✳ ————

We are living in a time where the kingdom model of marriage has almost become a rare breed. The divorce rate of Christians is at an all time high; the sad thing is, there are many broken marriages that could have been saved only if they would have implemented the word of the Lord in learning how to walk as one flesh and value the other over themselves.

My prayer is for this book to be a resource that strengthens and provide biblical and practical education to broken marriages and relationships and to provide direction to those seeking to have a healthy marriage and wholesome family structure.

The Purpose

The purpose of this book is to be a *unique resource tool* that the husband and wife can study together and apply in their daily lives. It is structured for teaching marriage workshops, singles' classes, and especially for those who are preparing themselves for this marriage journey.

As You Journey

As you journey through this book, you will notice it is not filled with stories, but my goal is to introduce to the readers specific topics and biblical principals that will not only challenge, strengthen, and bring understanding to many areas that marriages face, but it will produce strong families and healthy churches, which in turn produces strong communities.

My prayer is there will be many families saved and marriages restored because they dared to apply the kingdom principals that are in this resource material.

"Whoso findeth a wife findeth a good thing, and obtaineth favour of the Lord." -Proverbs 18:22

Dedication

---❋---

I dedicate this book first to my wonderful wife Yvette of thirty-four years, who has labored with me and is my strongest supporter in everything I put my hands to do. We have endured many tests and won many battles that challenged our covenant commitment, but we did not give up. Thank you sweetheart for always being a biblical model of strength, wisdom, and kingdom character. Because of my love commitment to you, I have obtained favor of the Lord. Thank you for trusting me with your whole heart. Love always.

To all married and engaged couples who have a desire to live a successful and fruitful marriage relationship that will stand the test of time.

To the couples who are finding challenges in their marriage relationship and are seeking applicable directions that will help them regain momentum in their marriage and strengthen the family structure.

To singles who are looking for material that will help them understand the dynamics of a marriage relationship and how to equip themselves for their future role as a husband or wife.

Table of Contents

❋

Introduction		vii
Dedication		ix
Chapter 1	The Ultimate Choice	13
Chapter 2	7 Marriage and Premarital Points	17
Chapter 3	Vision	23
Chapter 4	5 Strengths of Vision	25
Chapter 5	God's Order in Marriage	29
	God's Order Broken Down	32
Chapter 6	The Power of Walking Together	37
	Let's Go for a Walk	38
	The First Walk	42
	Walking Together as One Flesh	43
Chapter 7	Spiritual Intimacy	51
Chapter 8	Sex in Marriage	55
Chapter 9	Repairing the Gates of Your Marriage	61
Chapter 10	Love	65
Chapter 11	Practical Topics for Marriage Enrichment	67
Acknowledgments		77
About the Author		79
Bibliograpy		81

Chapter 1

The Ultimate Choice: A True Commitment

One of the greatest witnesses of true love is when a man and woman from different backgrounds and upbringing come together and commit their lives to one another.

They *choose* to live by the covenant standards of the Word of God and to achieve the ultimate goal of marriage, to become one flesh."

They understand they are different, and they must leave their father and mother and cleave one to the other. They also know to expect surprises and to seek God together. No matter what, they *choose* to make a commitment to marriage. They *choose* to model after the right couples and evaluate their relationship often. Respect, honor, and communication will be in the forefront of their relationship.

And the most important of all is to *put Christ first*.

Engaged or married, there are choices and commitments each person must make pre-marriage in order for there to be harmony and lasting joy in the relationship.

God has given us a manual to follow: the Bible. Somewhere along the journey, men and women tend to forget when they are faced with obstacles and challenges in marriage that they have a resource that will help them overcome anything.

It is time to challenge ourselves to change the way we have been dealing with marriage challenges that have not produced positive outcomes.

Marriage is work; therefore both parties must invest in making it work.

You know the old saying; "if you want to get different results, you must do something different."

With all the resources on how to make your marriage work, the question we need to ask ourselves is: why is the divorce rate so high?

Why do people choose not to take advantage of all the resources that are available? The answer is broad, but we do not have to fall victim to a bad marriage.

Have you made the Ultimate Choice?

Notes

What are some choices you may need to change to enhance your marriage?

_____
_____
_____
_____
_____
_____

Marital Points

Marital points are designed to give couples understanding of certain critical areas that they will face before and during their marriage. By no means is this *every* area, but key areas that need to be evaluated and discussed before and during marriage.

Chapter 2

7 Marriage and Premarital Points

Two different people – After the honeymoon is over and you begin to start this marriage journey, you notice things about your spouse that starts to make you think, Ok, I didn't know that? Don't be surprised, you must realize that you will never know everything about your spouse during courting time. That's why it's very critical that in the beginning stages of courting, learn as much as you can about each other's past, upbringing, thoughts on certain issues and lifestyles. (*A courtship of lust will blind you to real issues*)

One of the areas of challenge during your first five years of marriage is understanding and adjusting to the differences with which each one of you were created. Each spouse is not only different physically, but there are differences in backgrounds, habits, how to raise kids, outlook on life, and how to approach challenges.

One of the mindsets many people enter into a marriage is; we often think that after I marry this individual, that gives me the power to **CHANGE** them. Wrong, God designed those differences for a reason. And in a marriage relationship, we must learn that I'm not in this to change you, but through our uniqueness, we will learn how to walk in agreement and become One Flesh.

The more any couple learns to adjust to the other's uniqueness, and learn how to make those unique qualities to balance out your relationship, the stronger the marriage will become. This is part of making the Ultimate Choice!

Leave and cleave principal: Cut the cord. God gave this valuable principal for a reason, as it was spoken in three passages of Scripture: Genesis 2:24, Ephesians 5:31, Mark 10:1-9.

It is critical that you understand this principal in the beginning stages of marriage counseling and throughout the engagement process. To ignore this principal is to invite turmoil into your marriage. It's amazing that some refused to break that parental control over their marriage and needless to say, the marriage is shattered and the children are impacted tremendously.

Scripture lets us know one of the key transitions to becoming one flesh is to relinquish that parental tie and cleave to your spouse. That does not mean you no longer have anything to do with your parents, that means you are no longer under their authority, but you now belong to your spouse and your first responsibility of commitment and obligation is to your spouse and then your kids. Even your best friend now has to take a back seat to your spouse. As you will see later in this book, there is a kingdom structure that, if followed, will bring great success to your covenant relationship.

The "leave and cleave" principal applies to father, mother, children, siblings, and best friends. Decide in advance that no one, related or otherwise, is going to be a wedge between you two. This does not mean you disregard any helpful nuggets of wisdom.

Don't allow others to control the marriage vision you and your spouse have created for your marriage with their thoughts and ideas. You are no longer under the rule of your parents or best friends. You belong to each other. *Learn how to solve issues behind closed doors first. No one should know all your business!*

Genesis 2:24
Leave- heb- 5800- *azab* (aw-zab) prim root: to loosen, relinquish
Cleave-heb 1692- *dabaq* (daw-bak) root: cling or adhere, catch by pursuit, follow close (hard after), be joined together, abide, pursue hard

Expect surprises: when the honeymoon is over and things settle down, then the journey begins. There will be hard days, whether self-induced or life-induced. Life will always bring challenges, and those times have the ability to catch even the strongest marriages off guard if no one is prepared for them. We can never be fully prepared for what might come, but we can prepare ourselves that when the challenges come, whatever it is and no matter how hard it is, we will handle it together. These are the times couples must improve the strength of their marriage rather than allow them to pull the marriage apart.

How you approach surprises together will determine the success of victory or reveal the lack of preparedness on both of your parts.

Make a commitment to the marriage no matter the obstacles: When you stand before God and repeat your vows, you are making a solemn promise that whatever challenges come, you are not going to abandon your marriage and family, but you will stand side by side with your spouse and fight until you are victorious.

A lot of marriages have been abandoned because couples experienced hard times and challenges that caught them off guard. Marriage is more than simply being in love; it is a commitment to love, for better or worse, from that day forward. Verbalizing and agreeing to that on the front end, and *continuing to remind yourself* of that through the difficult days will make the marriage last. Ask for help soon, and don't let problems in the marriage linger too long, as that can prevent the worst scenario. Do not allow pride to keep you from asking for professional counseling if necessary. It's better to get help early than to wait too late and see the marriage fall apart beyond repair. Continue to strengthen each other when challenges come and remind yourselves that this little mountain will only make you stronger and bring you closer.

Model after the right couples: We often encourage couples to find a stable and mature couple whose marriage they admire and follow them closely. Ask questions about how they overcame obstacles and the keys to their successful relationship. Most likely, they have stories that will astound you.

No doubt they have learned to utilize biblical principals and the end result is having a strong marriage. This doesn't mean to pattern your marriage after theirs, but using it as a model relationship from which you can glean.

Always be open to correction and criticism by them; this will help you transition from a struggling or mediocre marriage to a strong and fruitful marriage. This can also prevent you from making future mistakes that could damage your marriage.

Marriage Evaluation: Establish the understanding early in the relationship that you have the right to periodically check on the state of your marriage. Couples should ask themselves often, "Are we growing closer together as a couple or further apart? Is the marriage growing stronger or are there broken gates that need repairing?" Don't assume your spouse feels as you do, ask each other if there are areas to change or improve.

These are times that you must be transparent and honest with each other. Always evaluate the character in which you are transparent and honest. Let it be done in love.

This is called *communication*: one of the most important tools in marriage. If you fail at this, you will surely miss issues that can lead to serious problems.

Christ must be first: It's the best application to a lasting marriage. Ecclesiastes 4:12 (NLT): "A person standing alone can be attacked and defeated, but two can stand back-to-back and conquer. Three are even better, for a triple-braided cord is not easily broken."

A spouse standing alone can be attacked and defeated, but two can stand together and endure the hardest days of a marriage. This is a statistical fact: when the relationship with Christ suffers, the marriage will often suffer and then the family. It is critical that you worship together in the same ministry. Some couples today feel it is okay to worship in different ministries. I believe it is important to attend the same house of worship because as a family, you should be worshipping together, and, you should be getting the same spiritual diet and spiritual direction. There must be a oneness, even in spiritual growth.

Satan looks for any excuse to divide a marriage. Pour your heart and life into Christ as one unit and let Him strengthen and sustain your marriage.

Notes

From the 7 Marital Points, which one/s do you feel you can improve on? Which ones have helped you and why?

_____
_____
_____
_____
_____
_____
_____
_____
_____
_____
_____
_____
_____

Chapter 3

Vision

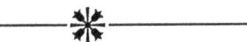

What is a Marriage Vision?

Many married couples have not been exposed to the notion of a vision for their marriage; in fact, vision is critical in marriage. Have you ever visualized what you would like your marriage to be? Happy, nice home, close knit family living in a nice neighborhood, you and your spouse traveling and doing fun things together, you rubbing his feet after a long days work, you making sure she is happy and has everything she needs. Believe it or not, that is a vision. Even though you may or may not have written it down, it was visualized in your mind and thoughts and you created a picture of it. That is what a vision is: the ability to think about or plan the future with imagination or wisdom; a mental image of what the future will or could be like.

As you learn more about visions, you will see and understand how valuable visions are when you incorporate it into your marriage and your own personal life.

When you can see and communicate your vision, it makes it easier to put into motion the things necessary to fulfill it.

There are several things you might want to consider in putting your marriage vision together. The most important thing is for the husband and the wife to come together and discuss what they each visualize the marriage to be and secondly, how is that achieved?

As you will discover in the Five Strengths of Vision, there are certain strengths that are needed to help make vision happen and allow you two to experience the joy in pursuing your marriage vision.

Habakkuk 2:2-3 (KJV): "And the Lord answered me, and said, 'Write the vision, and make it plain upon tables, that he may run that readeth it. For the vision is yet for an appointed time, but at the end it shall speak, and not lie: though it tarry, wait for it; because it will surely come, it will not tarry.'"

Utilizing this principal from the book of Habakkuk to write the vision helps the couple achieve an objective in their marriage, and it stands as a reminder to work toward that specific marriage goal. In the end, it will speak to others and be a testimony to them.

Below I have given you five virtues (strengths) of vision.

You will discover there is purpose and destiny housed in vision.

As you study these Scriptures, virtues, and definitions, apply them in your marriage as well as your personal life.

Five Strengths of Vision
Habakkuk 2:2-3 Write the vision
Proverbs 29:18 Without a vision

Chapter 4

5 Strengths of Vision

1. **Clarity:** clearness, free from doubt
2. **Passion and Energy**–an eagerness to make it happen
3. **Foresight**: When you don't have a vision it's hard to get excited
4. **Unity**: Making it happen together.
5. **Provision for the vision**: When executing the vision, the two of you must provide what is needed to carry out the vision.

Your assignment is for the two of you to come together and write out your marriage vision, frame it, and put it in a place where you will see it and always be reminded.

Note: As a marriage grows, so does the vision. As the marriage matures, the vision changes.

Below you will see "vision" broke down from *Strong's Exhaustive concordance,* Certain keywords have been broken down for further understanding. Your responsibility is to study these words as you write out your marriage vision.

Vision-heb 2377- *chazown* (khaw-zonezo: a sight (mentally) a dream, revelation from 2372- *chazah* (khaw-zaw) prim root- to gaze at; mentally to perceive, contemplate with pleasure, behold, prophesy, provide, see

Revelation- a new testament word Greek-602- *apokalupsis* (ap-ok-al-oop-sis): manifestation, be

revealed, lighten, from 601- to take off the cover

Proverbs 29:18 (NIV): "Where there is no revelation, people cast off restraint; but blessed is the one who heeds wisdom's instruction."

Vision allows you to have a targeted goal that you strive for to produce a future outcome that will be beneficial for the visionaries.

Notes

Do you think having a marriage vision could help in your marriage? Why or why not?
What are some of your marriage goals?

_____
_____
_____
_____
_____
_____

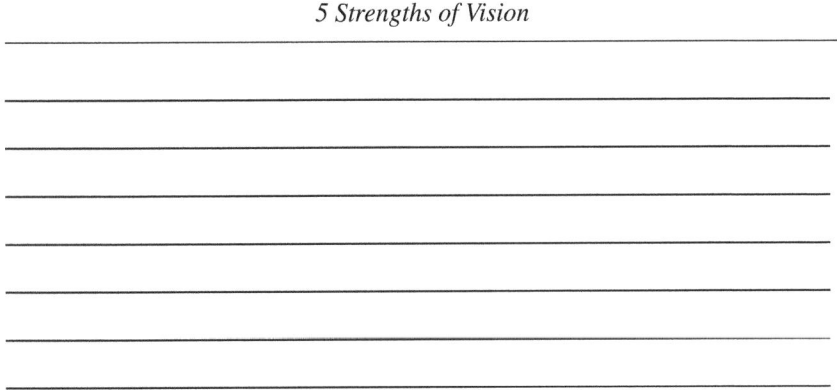

The Bible is specific on how we must conduct ourselves when married.

Not only does it gives us the tools on how to live successful in marriage, but God gives us a kingdom order that if followed, will produce a balanced and fruitful marriage.

As we can see, the world has allowed society to dictate what is order in a marriage relationship instead of what the Bible says about it.

This is one reason the divorce rate is so high, even in the kingdom. Couples, for whatever reason, refuse to follow God's divine blueprint for a successful covenant relationship.

As we will learn in this section, there is success in flowing God's way. When we approach marriage any way other than God's way, our families, as well as kingdom assignments, suffer.

In this chapter of God's order in marriage, look closely at how God gives specific direction on how each spouse is to serve one another. When we live in kingdom order, we will reap the benefits that come along with obedience. As you study Ephesians 5:22-33, there should be a greater understanding of how to serve one another in your marriage covenant.

Not only will you learn how to serve one another, but also you will learn the proper kingdom family structure:

God/personal relationship
Husband
Wife
Children/family
Ministry

Chapter 5

God's Order In Marriage

Ephesians 5:22-33 (NIV):

> Wives, submit yourselves to your own husbands as you do to the Lord. For the husband is the head of the wife as Christ is the head of the church, his body, of which he is the Savior. Now as the church submits to Christ, so also wives should submit to their husbands in everything. Husbands, love your wives, just as Christ loved the church and gave himself up for her to make her holy, cleansing her by the washing with water through the word and to present her to himself as a radiant church without stain or wrinkle or any other blemish, but holy and blameless. In this same way, husbands ought to love their wives as their own bodies. *He who loves his wife loves himself.* After all, no one ever hated their own body, but they feed and care for their body, just as Christ

does the church for we are members of his body. "For this reason a man will leave his father and mother and be united to his wife, and the two will become one flesh."

This is a profound mystery, but I am talking about Christ and the church. However, each one of you also must love his wife as he loves himself, and the wife must respect her husband.

In order for you to submit one to another, there must first be a submission to Christ and the kingdom order of God from both parties.

As this chapter begins with specific instructions of submission and marriage structure, God is giving us a parallel picture of how our marriage is suppose to mirror Christ's relationship with the church. If we follow these valuable principals, we will have great success in our covenant relationship.

Key Points in this Scripture
*Wives, submit to your own husbands as you do Christ
*The husband is the head of the wife
*Christ is the head of the husband
*Husbands, love your wife as Christ loves the church
*Husbands, wash your wife with the water of the Word
*Husbands, love your wife as your own body
*Wives, respect your husband

Submission and love is the kingdom formula for marital success!

Greek definitions from *Strong's Exhaustive Concordance:*

Submit: Greek 5293- *hupostasso* (hoop-ot-as-so): to subordinate, to be under obedience, submit self to. from 5259- *hupo* (hoop-o): a prime prep, (under) this word deals with to place or position

Head: Greek 2776- *kephal-* (kef-al-ayre): the head, a corner stone, uniting two walls; head, ruler, lord.

Cleansing: Greek 2511- *katharizo* (kath-ar-id-zo): make clean, purify, purge; from 2513- *katharso* (kath-ar-os): clean, clear, pure

Wash: Greek 3067- *loutron* (loo-tron): a bath / from 3068- a prime verb: to bath the whole person, baptize (this word is a form of spiritual covering)

Submission and love are the key components to a successful and strong marriage. Submission is not a bad word or controlling word; it is a voluntary position (not demeaning) one chooses to put themselves.

Submitting first to the word of the Lord and secondly to one another.

Loving one another as Christ loves you and gave himself for you.

If a man truly loves his wife, he loves himself. If a man does not love himself, he cannot love his wife.

God's Order Broken Down

God first: Putting God as number one in your life is your first and foremost priority. This is your personal relationship with God. We should never allow our spouse to hinder our personal relationship with God. Also, we cannot spend all of our time pursuing God and neglect our spouse; there must be a balance.

On the flip side, we should never be guilty of hindering our spouse from maintaining their personal relationship with God. One spouse not as motivated as the other can cause this, so they try to hinder the other by guilt, not giving them space to study or pray, among others. Loving God first will allow you to love one another.

Husband second: The husband is the spiritual and natural leader. He is to lead his family toward the kingdom, cover, protect, provide vision and structure for his family according to God's blueprint. He is to treat his wife as the Queen she is. Model the character of Christ and respects his wife as the one who is ordained to cover him and assist him in daily living and decision making. He works to take care of his family. His heart is tender towards the needs of his wife first and then the children.

He does not put his personal needs over his wife's needs and he looks to God for direction and instruction.

Wife third: The wife is the help meet. She walks alongside the husband in submission to his godly authority and assists him in whatever area is needed. She takes care of the home and kids and is the freshness of her home. She is wise and knows how to multitask. She trusts in the leadership of her husband and knows she has a voice in decisions that will affect the family. She is that prayer covering for her husband. She does not put her needs or the kids' needs over her husband's needs. She is the wisdom that holds the family together.

Children/Family fourth: Children and family are next and should not be put before the husband, wife, or God in the structure of order.

Too many times spouses have put kids before their marriage and the marriage suffers because of unbalanced structure. Scripture never mentions kids in the top three areas of kingdom structure, but the children are addressed in Chapter 6 of Ephesians. This is especially difficult to balance in blended families. As a blended family, if you do not receive wise counsel beforehand, you will have many conflicts that will wreck your home. Never—I repeat, *never*—put your kids before your spouse.

Teach both set of kids together about the family structure and let them know they will not play one parent against the other. You must trust your spouse when it comes to discipline. This is an area in blended families that can create serious marriage issues if not structured early in your marriage. No one parent should be the disciplinary of their own kids, but you are now a family and the discipline must be shared by both parents.

This is true for a spouse who is not the biological parent. Establish it early in your marriage and be consistent, hug, kiss, and be affectionate in front of them. *Never* put your spouse down in front of the children.

Ministry lastly: 1 Timothy 5:8 (NLT): "But those who won't care for their relatives, especially those in their own household, have denied the true faith. Such people are worse than unbelievers."

One area in marriage that is rarely ministered to is the area when the husband or wife is in a ministry position.

Ministry is being part of any auxiliary or five-fold office that requires your time at any given moment out side of the local church service, such as praise team, pastoral, elder, or musician.

As we are learning about godly order, let's keep in mind that building your marriage and family has priority over any position you may have in the local church.

Many leadership marriages have been jeopardized due to lack of kingdom order. That is why there are many kingdom leadership marriages suffering neglect due to misplaced priorities.

I have learned firsthand that it is so easy to get caught up in church things and unknowingly have a marriage that is on the brink of disaster. Praise God for my wife who brought it to my attention after enough was enough. A lesson well learned!

Deuteronomy 24:5 When a man is newly married, he shall not go out with the army or be liable for any other public duty. He shall be free at home one year to be happy with his wife whom he has taken.

This scripture is a clear indication even in the old testament that God had established kingdom order in marriage so there could be harmony, and a period for the newlyweds to set structure in the home.

We must balance ourselves to the point where ministry does not neglect our marriage or family.

As your marriage matures, you will be more flexible to extend yourself in ministry.

Remember, this principal can be applied to careers. If your career has taken priority over your family, you are "out of order"

Anything outside of this order is disorder:

God/personal relationship
Husband
Wife
Children/Family
Ministry

Notes

Is your family suffering because you are putting church over your family?

What happens when the family structure is out of balance?

If your job or career has caused division in your marriage, are you willing to make some adjustments?

Chapter 6

The Power of Walking Together

Introduction

We are living in a time where marriages are failing and families are falling apart by the numbers. God's heart is saddened to see all the marriages that have dissolved because the husband and wife did not understand the power of walking together. This section is designed to help the husband and wife discover more powerful tools that will help them reach a level of joy and peace in their marriage covenant and obtain a place of strength in their relationship and communication.

Yvette and I have proven this to be true after thirty-four years of marriage. Learning how to walk together in covenant relationship in the natural and in the spirit has blessed us to be able to minister to couples, not only by principals, but also by our lifestyle. The key to walking together successfully is agreement. When walking in the spirit of agreement, you create a spiritual flow and harmony that creates that "one flesh" unity the Bible speaks of. If Jesus desires for the church to walk in agreement with Him, how much more does He require for marriages to follow the same pattern?

A key to walking in a powerful and successful marriage is to understand *each* of you have the *ability* to *influence* the course of your marriage because of choice. Choice allows you the ability of selecting or making the proper decision when faced with difficult challenges. It's up to the two of you to walk in harmony and be in agreement, which in turn will influence the outcome of your marriage journey. Remember: your marriage does not have to end up like other destroyed marriages. You now have keys to a wholesome and peaceful marriage, so walk together in the covenant authority you have and experience marriage like it is meant to be.

If you talk the talk, you have to walk the walk!

Let's Go for a Walk

One of our best times of relaxation and courting is when we go for a love walk. It is a time of refreshing, peace, and bonding.

Some of the greatest times Yvette and I have are when we go walking. It brings us closer in many different ways: we take pictures, talk about God's handy work, encourage each other on our fitness goals, and it gives us a sense of adventure. We love walking during every season.

You can find so many benefits in taking walks together; you just have to start. Walking together brings a sense of harmony, security, intimacy, and so many other positive results. Hopefully by now, you have a better viewpoint on how taking walks can enhance a marriage relationship.

For the readers who have never had an interest in taking walks, stir up the adventure side of you that has been dormant and do something different that may enhance your marriage. As stated before, there are many healthy benefits in taking walks.

Now that you are motivated, excited, and stirred up to go on this new marriage adventure, here are some starting tips for you.

1. One thing we do for our adventures is look up parks and walking trails that we would like to visit. (You can also start in your neighborhood.) Most parks have walking trails with beautiful scenery; find a park and go. Our favorite times are early in the morning and later in the evening where taking pictures are the best. You pick what's best for you. We love getting up early when the sun rises, it is so peaceful, and watching the colorful sunset in the evening.
2. When walking, don't act as if you don't have anything in common, engage in some type of positive conversation. Treat this time as your special romantic time together. The more you put into it, the more you will get out of it. Husbands, it's always good for you to start the party. A lot of husbands don't know how to initiate a conversation, so usually it's one sided. Tell her how much you enjoy her company and how beautiful she is, sing a love song to her. In other words, make it fun. You must create the atmosphere for this special time of togetherness. Hold hands. This is not a time for pride or manhood issues; treat this time as an opportunity to engage in relationship building.

3. Wives, this is not a time of negativity or complaining, but a time to encourage and affirm your husband. Remember, this is a time of courting and bonding. Engage in your love language and if need be, show him how to engage in an intimate walk. Too many days go by that we get caught up in work, kids, and other obligations that we neglect spending *quality* time together. That is one of the silent marriage killers.

➤ Walks don't have to be long, but make them memorable

You determine the length of your walks. As you start enjoying them, they will get longer and longer.

I pray these few tips will help you start your quest on the power of walking together.

If walking is not applicable because of health reasons, you can use the principals for taking drives. Don't make excuses; just *get out of the house*!

Notes

If you have started your love walk because of this chapter, journal it and how it benefited you.

_____
_____
_____
_____
_____
_____
_____
_____
_____
_____
_____
_____
_____
_____
_____
_____
_____
_____
_____
_____
_____
_____
_____

The First Walk

The first walk recorded in the Bible is found in Genesis 3:8: "And they heard the voice of the Lord walking in the garden in the cool of the day: and Adam and his wife hid themselves from the presence of the Lord God among the trees of the garden."

The word "walk" in this verse comes from the Hebrew word *halak* (haw-lak): 1980 prime root- to be conversive, be at the point, lead, walk to and fro, up and down, to places.

From 3212- *yalak* (yaw-lak): prime root- pursue, cause to run.

Understand this is not the first recorded conversation God had with Adam, but the first recording of anything walking in the Scriptures.

It is amazing to me that it just so happens to be God's voice walking with husband and wife in the cool of the day.

Can you picture you and your spouse taking those love walks, and all of a sudden, God's voice starts walking with you? What an amazing experience that would be.

God's voice has always been walking in the earth trying to lead marriages in the right direction. Yet, sometimes we are like Adam and Eve; when there is a violation, we start the finger-pointing.

Our violations happen in the areas of selflessness, unfaithfulness, adultery, pride, lack of communication, no intimacy, and many other marriage violations. Like Adam and Eve, we always tend to blame each other for covenant violations instead of accepting our part and confessing our faults so there can be healing and restoration.

I believe God's voice is pursuing someone reading this right now, to the point that you are actually trying to cover up your marriage violations with the religious leaves. This is a time to fall on your knees and ask God for forgiveness, and then ask your spouse for forgiveness. There's healing in honesty and transparency.

God's voice walking in our marriage simply means we allow Him to lead our marriage through the Holy Spirit's guidance and His word. He is always trying to converse with us, but we must be open to what we wants to say about our marriage decisions. He will lead, but we must follow.

Even as Adam and Eve were privy to having God's voice walk with them and giving them instruction on how to walk as one flesh, we also have the same opportunity to experience God's voice walking with us in the cool of the day.

As we are walking on this journey, we must partner with God and His Word in order to ensure our steps are ordered by Him and He delights in our ways (Psalm 37:23).

Yvette and I have learned when we allow God's voice to walk with us, we do not have to hide, but in our nakedness and obedience, we can enjoy the benefits of marriage to its fullest.

When you began to walk as one flesh, you will began to walk in your God-given purpose as a husband and wife.

Walking Together as One Flesh

Walking together as one flesh is the pinnacle of the marriage relationship for which we all should strive. There are many things that will distract us on this marriage journey, and many mountains we will have to speak to along the way, but we must have a determination and commitment that we are going to walk together and have a vision-filled marriage that will stand the test of time, no matter what.

Too many times, our marriage walk is unbalanced. Instead of walking together, one is walking ahead of the other or we are going in different directions (blurred vision). The closer we walk together, the more we will become one flesh.

"One flesh" is that spiritual unity that not only brings you closer in the natural, but brings you closer in the spirit. It's that oneness that allows you to have a single vision and purpose and fulfill God's purpose for your lives so you can be one in all things.

God's role in the life of Israel was not only as their God, but also as a husband. He often communicated His heart to Israel in marriage language. In these passages of Scripture, examine the marital relationship God has with Israel and remember God sees our marriage in the natural just as His relationship with Israel and the church.

Ezekiel 16:8-14:

> "Then I passed by you and saw you, and behold, you were at the time for love; so I spread My skirt over you and covered your nakedness I also swore to you and entered into a covenant with you so that you became Mine," declares the Lord God. "Then I bathed you with water, washed off your blood from you and anointed you with oil. I also clothed

you with embroidered cloth and put sandals of porpoise skin on your feet; and I wrapped you with fine linen and covered you with silk.

"I adorned you with ornaments, put bracelets on your hands and a necklace around your neck. "I also put a ring in your nostril, earrings in your ears and a beautiful crown on your head. "Thus you were adorned with gold and silver, and your dress was of fine linen, silk and embroidered cloth you ate fine flour, honey and oil; so you were exceedingly beautiful and advanced to royalty. "Then your fame went forth among the nations on account of your beauty, for it was perfect because of My splendor which I bestowed on you," declares the Lord God.

Jeremiah 31:32: "'Not like the covenant which I made with their fathers in the day I took them by the hand to bring them out of the land of Egypt, My covenant which they broke, although I was a husband to them,' declares the Lord."

Isaiah 54:5: "For your husband is your Maker, Whose name is the Lord of hosts; and your Redeemer is the Holy One of Israel, Who is called the God of all the earth."

Jeremiah 3:20: "'Surely, as a woman treacherously departs from her lover, So you have dealt treacherously with Me, O house of Israel,' declares the Lord."

Isaiah 54:6-8:

> "For the Lord has called you, like a wife forsaken and grieved in spirit, Even like a wife of one's youth when she is rejected," says your God. "For a brief moment I forsook you, but with great compassion I will gather you. In an outburst of anger I hid My face from you for a moment, but with everlasting loving-kindness I will have compassion on you," says the Lord your Redeemer.

Revelation 19:7-9:

> Let us rejoice and be glad and give the glory to Him, for the marriage of the Lamb has come and His bride has made herself ready. It was given to her to clothe herself in fine linen, bright and clean; for the fine linen is the righteous acts of the saints. Then he said to me, "Write, 'Blessed are those who are invited to the marriage supper of the Lamb.'" And he said to me, "These are true words of God."

Can two people who have committed their lives together as covenant soul mates walk as one flesh if they are not in agreement?

As God's desire for Israel was to have a strong covenant relationship with him, they first had to learn the consequences of braking covenant, and value the one who is always faithful.

Amos 3:3 (KJV): "Can two walk together, except they be agreed?"

As I have broken down what walking together in agreement is according to the Hebrew language, closely examine the three keywords in Amos 3:3: "walk," "together," and "agreed."

Walk: Heb- 3212 *yalak* (yaw-lak'): root- flow, follow, grow, prosper, be weak

Together: Heb- 3162-*yachad* (yakh'-ad): a unit, alike

from- 3161 *yachad* (yaw-khad'): prime root- to be(or become one) join, unite

One- Heb- 259 *echad* (ekh-awd): united, alike from 258 *achad* (aw-khad): prime root- to unify; the number denoting unity, being the same in kind and quality

Agreed Heb- 3259- *ya'ad* (yaw-ad'): root- to engage (for marriage) betroth

    I have combined most of the definitions in sentence form to give you an idea of what it means to walk in agreement.
    Walking in agreement and becoming one flesh happens by pursuing greatness through the power of influence God has placed inside of you, and producing a systematic rhythm as a covenant team. You must keep your attention fixed on God's divine direction for your lives. This will cause you to achieve maturity and economic success, not being weak or impotent

in your walk, but a well-oiled covenant unit equal in love and commitment being unified as one flesh.

When you walk as one flesh, you are engaged in a seamless flow, which produces harmony of daily living and a strong family structure, because you realize in order for you to become one flesh, there must be harmony in everything you do.

When walking together as one flesh, there is no weakness in your marital structure, but power and strength that will produce the vision and affect the seven marital points.

Notes

Have you ever noticed God's voice walking in your marriage?
What has He said?
Now that you have studied how to walk as one, do you have a better concept of the power of being one? Explain.

Chapter 7

Spiritual Intimacy

Spiritual intimacy is a key component in a covenant relationship. Spiritual intimacy is a sense of unity and mutual commitment to God's purpose for our lives and marriage, along with a respect for the special dreams of each other's hearts. It's one of the greatest depths of intimacy we experience in marriage.

It's important get a clear understanding of intimacy in order for us to effectively implement Spiritual Intimacy. First and foremost, intimacy does not apply only to sex. Intimacy is defined as: close familiarity or friendship; a private cozy atmosphere, an intimate remark. The **Thesaurus** defines intimacy as: closeness, togetherness, rapport, attachment, familiarity, friendliness, friendship, affection, warmth, confidence; sexual relations, (sexual) intercourse, lovemaking;

One definition that sticks out to me is the word rapport. It means; a close and harmonious relationship in which the people or groups concerned understand each other's feelings or ideas and communicate well:

That's powerful!

Values are important in spiritual intimacy. This means we value God's purpose for our spouse's life and the dreams of their heart. A marriage is not consider balanced if one spouse is more important than the other.

A godly marriage happens when two people who are created in God's image join together to help each other fulfill God's calls on their lives.

When you value each other spiritually, you partner with God to help your spouse reach their spiritual potential. Evaluate how you value your spouse's needs, and if you put your needs before theirs.

Energy is fuel to spiritual intimacy. There must be a drive and passion in pursuing God as individuals and together as a couple. This means putting in the spiritual work. Apply energy to your spiritual life. Pray together, worship together, and seek God together. Encourage each other to pursue greatness in God. Iron sharpening iron.

Sacrifice is necessary to spiritual intimacy. This means sacrificing the desire to only promote yourself or worry about yourself. In other words, you give of yourself on the behalf of the other.

Both men and women have a natural selfishness. Without God's help, we would only care about ourselves. Spiritual intimacy will not occur unless we both put our own needs behind meeting the needs of our spouse.

When one spouse invests in their spouse's dreams over their own, it draws them closer and they will accomplish many great things because they are flowing biblically.

Finally, trust is key to spiritual intimacy. This means creating an atmosphere where you can share your deepest spiritual desires and dreams and so can your spouse. Once you've shared your dreams, your spouse must honor them, respect them, and treat them carefully.

Some of the deepest fights in a relationship occur from a dream or vision violation. Not trusting your spouse's dreams will not be beneficial for you and will eventually hurt the marriage and effect your spiritual intimacy. Do not disrespect or damage your spouses dreams.

In order to have spiritual intimacy in your marriage, you must *invest* in it.

One of the greatest investments is when you invest in your spouse looking for nothing in return.

Notes

How will you implement value, energy, sacrifice, and trust into your marriage?

Have you had dreams that have been killed by your spouse?

If so, have you discussed it with your spouse and how have you recovered?

Study the definitions of intimacy and share with your spouse the ones that impact you the most.

Chapter 8

Sex in Marriage

One of the greatest expressions in a marriage relationship is sexual intimacy. This is not a dirty word; God created sex for the fulfillment pleasure of a married couple. Not only to procreate, but to express a greater dimension of love.

As in God's original structure, sexual pleasure was created for a married man and married woman, but as we see all throughout the history of the earth, man has defiled this most precious gift and polluted it to the point where we have caused it to become vile and degraded.

Many marriages have been destroyed because the cultural society says you can have sex if you want to, regardless if it is with your own spouse or two men or two women. As married couples, we must live our marriage relationship with faithfulness and satisfaction. Don't allow the sexual vibes of society to lure you away from your most precious jewel (your spouse).

Keep the fire of you marriage fresh, learn what makes your spouse sexually aroused, and let them know if you are uncomfortable doing certain things. The bedroom experience should be a great experience and not a marriage porn experiment.

What does the Bible say?

Genesis 1:28: "God blessed them and said to them, 'Be fruitful and increase in number; fill the earth and subdue it.'"

1 Corinthians 7:1-5 (NIV):

> Now for the matters you wrote about: "It is good for a man not to have sexual relations with a woman." But since sexual immorality is occurring, each man should have sexual relations with his own wife, and each woman with her own husband. The husband should fulfill his marital duty to his wife, and likewise the wife to her husband. The wife does not have authority over her own body but yields it to her husband. In the same way, the husband does not have authority over his own body but yields it to his wife. Do not deprive each other except perhaps by mutual consent and for a time, so that you may devote yourselves to prayer. Then come together again so that Satan will not tempt you because of your lack of self-control.

Proverbs 5:15-19 (NLT):

> Drink water from your own well
> Share your love only with your wife.
> Why spill the water of your springs in the streets,
> having sex with just anyone?
> You should reserve it for yourselves. Never share
> it with strangers.
> Let your wife be a fountain of blessing for you.
> Rejoice in the wife of your youth.
> She is a loving deer, a graceful doe.
> Let her breasts satisfy you always.
> May you always be captivated by her love.

Hebrews 13:4 (NLT): "Give honor to marriage, and remain faithful to one another in marriage. God will surely judge people who are immoral and those who commit adultery."

KJV: "Marriage *is* honorable in all, and the bed undefiled: but whoremongers and adulterers God will judge."

Undefiled Greek- 283 *amiantos* (am-ee'eam-tos): untainted, free from contamination, pure, unsoiled

Never withhold sexual intimacy from one other as punishment.

Enhanced relationship/Non-Sexual Affection

When a husband only touches his wife only when he's ready for sex, it can easily cause her to feel used and not valued. Women express when affection and closeness (touching) is consistent within the marriage, it causes them to want more sex and to enjoy it more. Others say that if non-sexual touching were displayed more, it would put them in the mood and even cause them to be more aggressive and perhaps creative at bed time.

While all of the physical touching may not be initiated among couples, they can be added, as often as they choose, realizing how much more exciting and invigorating non-sexual touches can be. If the two of you are into touching each other, then you can be even more creative. Couples will experience a greater bonding and closeness as they incorporate some bundle of touches to their lifestyle.

When couples engage in non-sexual affection together, they feel more connected. Being touched by your mate keeps the fire burning, shows true intimacy, builds trust, creates transparency, and strengthens the relationship in various ways. Let's remember non-sexual affection does not take the place of sexual intercourse. It can, however, set the pace for leading to it, but that is not the intent.

Sexual touches relate to foreplay, manipulation, and stimulation leading to sexual intercourse. Having good sex keeps a relationship alive, exciting, and fresh. Sexual intercourse has its place, and so do non-sexual touches. Both should be indulged in regularly.

Make and Take Time

Couples must make and take time to enjoy being married. The busyness of life can cause marriages to lose their focus for each other and they no longer feel the connection they once shared. Raising children, the work place, social activities, religious commitments, illnesses, financial obligations, and you name it, can so easily become the center of attention. Let's be honest: planning, scheduling, and maintaining ways to fulfill the much-needed day to day challenges, somehow in the midst of it all, get taken care of. The item that never gets on the schedule is the two of you. That should never be.

Spending time together at a family activity, event, grocery shopping, or even arguing, is not the kind of quality time you spent together before marriage. Your focused was on each other more than anything else planning ways to enjoy one another. Most likely your relationship was deeply sparked by all types of touches.

Many couples have not touched for a long time, or do too little touching for various reasons. While it is difficult to imagine, some couples never touch; there is no intimacy in the relationship. You must make time!

Notes

Do you ever share with your spouse how you feel about your sexual experiences with them? Why not?

    Is talking about sex uncomfortable between you and your spouse? Why?

_____
_____
_____
_____
_____
_____
_____
_____
_____
_____
_____
_____
_____
_____
_____
_____
_____
_____
_____
_____
_____

Chapter 9

Gates of Your Marriage

I n this chapter, we want to look at spiritual gates and why it is important to keep them maintained.

Gates are the access points to your marriage house that, if not guarded and maintained, could allow many unwanted intruders in. The four main gates are: eyes, ears, heart, spirit. When these key gates are neglected and not guarded, the enemy of our souls will have a hay day in our marriage.

Now, in order for us to repair any gates, we must know there is damage. That is why I stated in Chapter 2 to evaluate your marriage often; when you do this, you will notice gates that need to be repaired.

In marriage, we are always building. No marriage is set or completely built, but there are always new challenges and life events that will reveal areas of your marriage that may need to be repaired.

Your responsibility is to daily examine your marriage structure and gates, and if there is any damage, immediately get your spiritual tool belt and repair that area.

Gates are spiritual access entrances to your marriage house.

How strong is your water gate?

The water gate is a picture of the Word of God and its effect in our lives. Water in the scriptures represents the Holy Spirit and cleansing. Scripture always parallels the marriage relationship with Christ's relationship with the church. Ephesians 5:25-26 states ... having washed her by the water of the word. This gate is important because the husband should be washing his spouse with the word. The Holy Spirit is the one who makes the Word of God alive to us personally, allowing cleansing, encouragement, and direction to take place in our daily life. Husbands, do not allow this gate to go un-repaired.

As kingdom covenant believers, you must not allow the water gate to become stagnant due to neglect and not allowing the rivers to become living in your personal lives as well as in your marriage, but strive together in the things of God, building each other in the word and often inviting the Holy Spirit to wash, cleanse, and purify your marriage.

(Stagnant water is a breading ground for insects!)

Repairing gates is not just for the husband, but for the wife also.

When there is a breech in our gates, it is because we have neglected to fix it or prolong repairs and the enemy walks right in; he knows when marriage gates are being neglected because he is constantly spying out our unity, and looks for any signs of neglect in our spirit gate first and then our eye gates, our mind gates, and our heart gates. If those gates are not fixed, he creeps right on in and creates havoc.

The marriage gate-crasher loves to show up to parties when these areas are jumping off:

*Selfishness (pride) *stubbornness *disrespect *tearing down *confusion *financial troubles *lack of intimacy *unfaithfulness *distrust *lack of communication

We cannot defeat the enemies of our marriage covenant if we neglect our broken gates. Keep up the maintenance on you marriage gates and be prayerful who you allow to have access through your gates.

Keep the light of the holy spirit shining on your marriage so every perimeter of your marriage house is lit up with the light of love and at every gate entrance is a welcome mat that reads "One Flesh Walking Together As One."

When a man does not know how to repair broken gates, he sometimes abandons his post.

Men, we cannot continue to run from challenges and leave our families uncovered, but we must meet every challenge head-on and look God in His face and cry for help.

Notes

What gates have you recognized as broken in your marriage? What tools have you used to repair any broken gates?

Chapter 10

Love

1 Corinthians 13:4-7 (NIV):

> Love is patient, love is kind. It does not envy, it does not boast, it is not proud. It does not dishonor others, it is not self-seeking, it is not easily angered, it keeps no record of wrongs. Love does not delight in evil but rejoices with the truth. It always protects, always trusts, always hopes, always perseveres. Love never fails. And now these three remain: faith, hope and love. But the greatest of these is love.

God's vision of love is totally different from the world's vision of love. When we understand this and put it into practice, we will experience a level of marital harmony and kingdom living that gives us an advantage that other relationships lack. This is the foundation to what every marriage must be built upon. One thing I have learned in my thirty-four years of marriage is when I love my wife like Christ loves the church, that same love will extend itself to other areas of my life, within the marriage and outside of the marriage.

The worlds 'view of love is usually based on conditions and sex.

As a married couple, it is needful to fully understand the many characteristics that are housed in God's law. When you understand the dynamics of love and apply them biblically, you will be able to stand the many tests and challenges that will present themselves along your marriage journey as well as in daily living.

Scripture tells us what love is and is not in 1 Corinthians 13:

It Protects
It Trusts
It Hopes
It Preserves
It never fails
*It neve*r disappoints
It never ceases to work well
It never: dies away
It never: becomes bankrupt
It never: deserts or let down (someone)

Agape love must be the foundation that every marriage is built upon.

Chapter 11

Practical Topics for Marriage Enrichment

※

Practical Topics is an exercise that the husband and wife participate in *together*. It is designed to reveal each spouse's thoughts on relationship topics that may not be discussed or thought about throughout the marriage relationship.

From the seventeen topics in bold, split them up between you two and expound on the topics as it relates to your marriage relationship. *Do this exercise separately.* When finished, come together in an intimate setting and share. Remember: the key to this exercise is to see what each spouse thinks about the topics as it relates your relationship. If there are any topics that you have not experienced, this would be a great time to innate them into your marriage.

Below is a copy of our first marriage enrichment exercise that was done years ago. It will give you some clarity on how to complete your assignment. Living out these marriage enrichment topics daily is what helps us keep our relationship strong.

We love being together. -Jimmy

We love it when we're together. That makes our marriage so much fun.

Spending time together and doing things together has enriched our marriage so much; we anticipate times when we can get away and hang out together. We pretty much know when we need to give the other some air. We don't smother one another. When you love being together, you are on your way to a successful marriage.

We remind ourselves often of what a great treasure our spouse is to us. -Jimmy

We often remind each other how much we value and treasure each other. We can never affirm one another too much. If you have a wonderful spouse, remind them how much of a treasure they are and cherish your treasure.

We both sincerely desire for our marriage to be a great marriage. -Jimmy

Oh yeah, there has been times of testing, frustration, and at one point, asking, are we going to make it? We both made up our minds that our marriage is worth saving because we love each other and see ourselves being together the rest of our lives. Having a vision of what you want your marriage to be is critical in the quest for a great marriage. For where your treasures are, there is your heart. If you treasure your marriage, your heart will be to do all you can to make it great.

We don't keep secrets from each other. -Jimmy

What's done in secret will come to light. This is a truth that will come to pass every time.

A healthy marriage is built on trust and openness. As we are entering into our thirty-fifth year of marriage, God has taught us to be open and true to each other. Anything that is hidden or concealed is a secret. My daily activities are an open book to my wife. She is my rib, my best friend, lover, and so much more.

Without trust, there will be secrets.

We treasure our getaways together. -Jimmy

We usually do not let anything stop us from our getaways. This is a time of anticipation, expectation, and fun. Getting on the road and visiting a city is our set aside time to get away from everything and do what we love doing, exploring different cities, parks, lakes and creating memories. Always set a yearly retreat where just you two can get away and enjoy each other. It's well worth it.

We use this technique when we are having a tough time communicating. -Jimmy

Every couple needs to find their own technique of communication when having trouble communicating. What we found helpful is to give each other space to process the issue, come back and discuss the problem in a civil manner. Rarely do we holler at each other. We have grown to know that shouting at each other just makes it worse.

Name-calling and leaving is a no no!

We try to keep a teachable spirit.-Jimmy

I love being able to teach my wife better ways to do things. But do you love when she tries to teach you a better way? This principal goes both ways. What is the best way that will accomplish the task at hand in spite of whose idea it was?

Yes I use to think for the most part that my way was the best way. I admit, I was controlling! Humility is a key to attaining a teachable spirit. You will be surprised how much you can learn from one another.

We believe it is important to have joint money accounts. -Jimmy

This is a controversial topic that stirs couples' juices. I am touching this topic because I want to share what works for others and us, and maybe it will help someone that might be struggling with this issue. Remember: what works for one may not work for others. But this is a topic that comes up in marriage counseling and we love sharing the positives about joint accounts.

Everyone wants to control their own money, right?

This is an area that can strengthen or destroy a marriage.

Every marriage should be built upon the "one flesh" concept; that includes every day living. Operating in this requires a relationship of trust and un-selfishness. We have learned if you can flow in this area of oneness, you are equipped to weather many storms.

Our finances are an open book. We have accounts with both names on them with ATM access. We never violate the other's account, but communicate if there is a need.

Our structure is, you manage yours and I manage mine, and if there is a need, it will be taken care of.

We enjoy sharing the details of life with each other. -Yvette

When I was in school I had a best friend Willa; we talked about everything. Anything good or bad that happened, she was the first person I called to share it with because I knew she had my back. God gave me a new best friend in Jimmy Mitchell; now when something good or bad happens, he's the first person I call and share it with, because we have that relationship of sharing and communication.

We have learned that the best way for our needs to be met is to make the other's happen. -Yvette

One of the first things I remember learning in preschool is The Golden Rule: Do unto others as you would have them do unto you. In practicing this principle, we learn not to be selfish. When my husband and I focus on serving one another, it brings joy to our marriage.

We enjoy letting other people know how much we love each other. -Yvette

I was in my cube at work when I overheard a co-worker speaking derogatorily of her husband. What a negative picture she painted of him and their marriage. I sat there and thanked God that people come to me and ask things like, "So what new adventures are Jimmy and Yvette up to?" I lift my husband up every chance I get. As we share our love for each other we are also sharing the love of Christ through us.

Close friends of the opposite sex can be dangerous. -Yvette

We are careful about how we relate to others of the opposite sex: we believe having too close of a relationship with the opposite sex is destructive. We always let it be known that our spouse is our one and only,

We treasure our "date times" together. -Yvette

Our date time is the best; it's real simple, nothing fancy. We go for love walks, sit outside on the patio and talk or enjoy a bonfire if the weather is right. This is what we call "our space." In our space, we laugh, cry, and share our heart.

We do everything we can to protect "our space." This is where we reconnect.

Sometimes we have to agree to disagree. -Jimmy

Sometimes we don't see eye to eye on every issue. After we have tried to discuss the issues completely and realize neither of us can persuade the other; at this point we know we have to let it go and go on loving each other even when we don't agree.. Just let it go!

We try to be sensitive to the "hurt vs. angry" issue. -Yvette

It is not unusual for one of us to think the other is angry when he/she is actually feeling hurt about something. In fact, it's not unusual for us to have these feelings at the same time. At these times we try to be sensitive at several points: First we know we have a spiritual enemy, the devil, who would like to mess up and confuse our communication. If he can make us misunderstand each other, he can do damage to our relationship.

Secondly, we try to remind ourselves that we cannot tell the other how to feel. If I'm accused of being mad when I'm hurt, it just makes the problem worse.

In those situations, if one of us can find the grace to apologize for getting angry, or for trying to tell the other how he/she feels (or should feel), or for not listening to the other carefully, we can usually take a lot of steam out of the situation pretty quickly.

We seriously keep the Lord Jesus Christ at the center of our marriage. -Yvette

We keep the Lord Jesus Christ at the center of our marriage fold. This cord is not easily broken and the only way we can do all things is with Jesus as the center core. Jesus as our core makes us accountable to each other and to our family. It helps us withstand the attacks from the enemy and temptation to sin.

We treat each other with the utmost respect. -Yvette

Another song comes to mind: "Respect" by Aretha Franklin. In this song, this woman is telling her man she will give him anything if he just respects her when he comes home! Respect means to give the feeling of esteem, to avoid violation, to value, to be polite and kind. Jimmy and I always try to use kind words like, "please," and "thank you," and we have no problem with the big one: I'm sorry.

It is never okay to dump on each other because we may have had a bad day nor is it okay to not be kind.

The strength of any community flows from strong families. Strong families are a product of healthy marriages.

In order for us to understand the importance of healthy marriages, let's evaluate our families and neighborhoods to see the effects broken homes have in our communities.

In order for any marriage relationship to be healthy and fruitful, the husband and wife must function as *one flesh*. Do not allow anything or anyone to lure you away from the covenant commitment you made with your spouse.

Just as Christ gave His life for all to reconcile man back to Himself, fight for your marriage; no matter what it may cost you.

Acknowledgments

I would like to first give praise to Jesus Christ my Lord for His unconditional love toward me and my family and for giving me the vision and passion for marriage ministry that has blessed many couples, including my own marriage.

To my wonderful and anointed wife, Yvette, for being my best friend in the storms and in the sunshine. You never cease to amaze me how you are always by my side lifting me up and making sure I have everything I need to fulfill my assignment on this earth. What an amazing woman!

To every couple who trusted us with your most intimate issues and allowed us to deposit seeds of healing and direction into your marriage.

To our best friends, Clarence and Helen Campbell, for being with us in the beginning stages of our marriage ministry over twenty years ago. Thanks for your continual support and wonderful friendship.

To Apostle Gary and Pastor Tosca Smith, thank you for your continual prayers and support of One Flesh Marriage Ministries and all that you do encourage Yvette and myself to walk in the full measure of what God has called us to do.

To Bishop Nathaniel Jordan, thank you for being a wonderful spiritual father and living example of what a wholesome kingdom marriage should look like. Even though God has called your best friend (Marta Jean) home, your marriage of sixty years will still impact the lives of many. We love you!

To my mother Catherine Gordon: Thank you for filling both roles as a mother and father to seven kids and always encouraging me to be the best in everything I do. Thanks for being a great example of a strong woman full of wisdom and love. As I have inherited your skills as a chef, I also inherited your skills in the Word of God. You are awesome! I love you to life!

About the Author

---❋---

Jimmy Mitchell is a native of Columbus, Ohio. A graduate of Columbus East High School, he studied electronics at ITT in Dayton, Ohio, and has worked in the culinary field for 25 years.

He has been married for thirty-four years to his wonderful wife, Yvette R. Mitchell, and is the proud father of four kids: three girls and one son with seven awesome grandchildren.

Growing up with six sisters and being the only male, he is a product of a single-parent home. Jimmy knows the pain of growing up without a father and experienced the father wounds of abandonment. That is why he is passionate about helping married couples reach their potential in becoming *one flesh*, and to help restore broken and damaged families.

Jimmy has served Christ for over twenty-five years and served in marriage ministry for twenty years. He is co-founder, along with his wife, of One Flesh Marriage Ministry of Columbus, Ohio, a marriage resource ministry that trains and equips couples to live a successful and rich marriage.

As an ordained elder, Jimmy oversees several ministries in the local church, and has a passion for mentoring young men who are fatherless.

Jimmy functions in a pastoral anointing and flows in the gift of teaching, training, and exhortation.

He is a mentor and father figure to many, helping them to become all that they can be in life and in the kingdom.

Bibliography

---✤---

Scripture verses come from The Holy Bible, New International Version, New Living Translation, King James Version Copyright 1973, 1984,

Scripture taken from the King James Version 1982 by Thomas Nelson

The Living Bible Copyright 1971 by Tyndale House Foundation

New Oxford American Dictionary and Thesaurus, September 2001, Oxford University Press

The Strong's Exhaustive Concordance of the Bible, James Strong 1822-1894, LL.D., S.T.D
Copyright 1990 by Thomas Nelson Publishers